SCIENCE EVERYWHERE!

Where Food Comes From

The Best Start in Science

By Ronne Randall

New
Forest
Press

First published in North America in 2010 by New Forest Press,
PO Box 784, Mankato, MN 56002
www.newforestpress.com

TickTock project editor: Rob Cave
TickTock project designer: Trudi Webb

ISBN 978-1-84898-294-9
Library of Congress Control Number: 2010925597
Tracking number: nfp0002
Printed in the USA
9 8 7 6 5 4 3 2 1

Picture credits (t=top, b=bottom, c=center, l=left, r=right,
OFC=outside front cover, OBC=outside back cover):

Alamy: 1tl, 8bl, 11c, 12r, 15tl, 18b, 19b, 20t, 20c, 20bl, 16c,
17 (background). Corbis: 1ct, 1tr, 1c, 2tl, 2tr, 3tl, 3tc, 4tl, 4cr, 5tl, 5tr, 6tl, 7tl, 7b,
10tl, 10tr, 10bl, 11b, 12tl, 13b, 16tl, 16b, 17t, 17bl, 19t, 20br, 21br, 22c, 22br
(orange), 24t, 24c, 24br (oranges). Photolibrary: 15c. Science Photo Library: 9tl.
Shutterstock: OFC all, 6b, 7tr, 10l, 14b, 22-23 (background), OBC all.

Contents

Any words appearing in the text in bold, **like this**,
are explained in the Glossary.

Have you ever wondered where the food you eat comes from?

The supermarket

The baker

The farm

Maybe your parents buy all your food at the grocery store. Maybe they get some from the baker, or the greengrocer, or even from the farm.

But have you ever wondered how the food gets there?

How is it made? What is it made from?

What are fries made from?

Fries are made from potatoes.
Potatoes grow in fields on farms.

Sprouting potatoes

When potatoes are quite old they start to sprout.

If you **plant** these potatoes in the ground each one will grow into a potato plant.

The potato plants will grow more potatoes!

The potatoes are ready to be dug up when the plants' leaves turn yellow.

Potatoes can be cut into fries, and cooked.

Enjoy your fries!

What food is made from tomatoes?

Ketchup is made from tomatoes. The tomatoes grow on plants.

Tomato plants grow in rows. Before they are **ripe** the tomatoes are green.

When the tomatoes are red they are ready to be picked.

Tomatoes are crushed in a **vat** at the ketchup factory.

A vat

The crushed tomatoes are mixed with salt, sugar, spices, and vinegar.

Do you like Ketchup on your burger and fries?

The mixture is cooked and put into bottles.

What is bread made from?

Bread is made from wheat.
Farmers plant wheat in fields.

Wheat
ear

As the wheat gets bigger an **ear** grows at
the top. This is where the wheat **grains** are.

At **harvest** time a
combine harvester
cuts down the wheat.
The grains are
separated from
the ear.

The grains are crushed to make flour. The flour is sold to bakeries and shops.

Flour

Grain

At the bakery, water, sugar and yeast are added to make **dough**.

The dough is baked in the oven…

…and here comes the bread.

Where do eggs come from?

Eggs come from hens. Hens are female chickens.

Chick

Hens eat lots of grain—about 80 pounds (36 kilograms) a year!

Grain

The eggs are collected and packed into cardboard cartons.

Next the eggs are sent to a **grading station**. They are washed and checked, to make sure they are not damaged.

Then the eggs are sorted by size and put in cartons.

The next stop is the shop, and then your breakfast table!

Which foods come from cows?

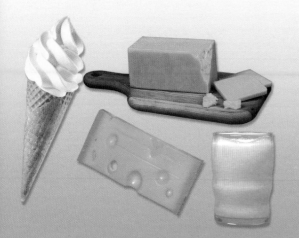

Butter, ice cream, yogurt, and cheese are all made from milk...

...and milk comes from cows!

Cows live on farms. They eat special feed and green grass.

Udder

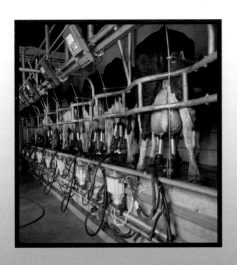

A milking machine is attached to the cow's **udder**. Milk comes out of the udder.

Some milk goes to factories to make cheese, yogurt, butter, and ice cream.

Then it is delivered to the grocery store, or to your doorstep!

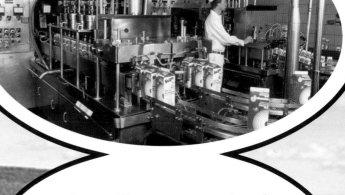

The milk is **pasteurized** in a **dairy** to kill any germs. The milk is poured into cartons and bottles.

Where does orange juice come from?

Orange juice comes from oranges.

Oranges are **fruits**, and they grow on trees.

The trees grow in places like Spain and in Florida, in the USA, where it is warm and sunny almost all year.

When they are ripe the oranges are harvested and taken to a factory.

The oranges are washed, then sent to the **extractors**, which squeeze out the juice.

The juice is pasteurized to kill germs.

It is poured into cartons and bottles. Drink up!

What kind of a plant is rice?

Rice is actually a kind of grass. It is a **cereal** plant.

Rice is grown in a field called a paddy. The paddy is flooded with water, about two to four inches (five to ten centimeters) deep.

When the rice is ready to be harvested it is picked by hand or by a machine.

The rice is dried and taken to a mill.

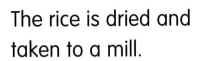

At the mill, the rice **kernels** are separated from the **husks**.

The rice kernels are sent to factories and are packed into bags, ready to be cooked!

19

What is chocolate made from?

Chocolate is made from cocoa beans. Cocoa beans are the **seeds** of the cacao tree fruit.

Cacao trees grow in warm, **tropical** countries like Brazil and Indonesia.

The fruits are picked, and the beans are left to dry in the Sun.

Cocoa beans

The dried cocoa beans are **roasted** and crushed into a **liquid**.

Chocolate paste

Sugar and milk are added to the liquid, and it is blended into a paste.

The paste is poured into **molds**.

As it gets cooler it goes hard.

Now the bars are ready for wrapping ... then unwrapping and eating!

Questions and answers

Q What goes well with fries and is made from tomatoes?

A Ketchup is made from tomatoes and goes well with fries.

Q Where do eggs come from?

A Eggs come from hens.

Q What is bread made from?

A Bread is made from wheat.

Q What fruits are made into juice?

A We can get juice from almost any fruit. The most popular fruit juices are orange, apple, grapefruit, grape, and pineapple.

Q Are tomatoes a fruit or a vegetable?

A Most people think tomatoes are vegetables, but actually they are fruits because they have seeds inside them.

Q What other animals make milk that people drink?

A Sheep and goats both make milk that people drink.

Q What kind of plant is rice?

A Rice is a kind of grass.

Q What is chocolate made from?

A Chocolate is made from cocoa beans.

Glossary

Cereal A grass whose grains are used for food.

Combine harvester A machine that cuts down cereal plants.

Dairy A place where milk is prepared before it is sold.

Dough A mixture of flour and water. It is baked into bread.

Ear The part of a cereal plant that holds the seeds.

Extractors Machines that remove or separate parts of something.

Fruits Foods like apples, oranges and pears that grow on plants, vines or trees. They have seeds inside them.

Grading station A place where eggs are sent to be checked and measured, before being sent to shops.

Grains The seeds of a cereal plant.

Harvest To pick or gather crops or fruit that are ready to eat.

Husks The outer shells of seeds. They are usually taken off and thrown away.

Kernels The parts of seeds that are inside the husks.

Liquid Something that is runny. Water is a liquid.

Molds Shaped containers that hold something while it hardens.

Pasteurized When milk or orange juice has been made very hot in order to kill germs.

Plant To put something in the soil so it can grow.

Ripe When a fruit or vegetable is fully grown and ready to be picked for eating.

Roasted To cook something in an oven until it is dry.

Seeds Small parts of a plant that can grow into a new plant.

Tropical A place where the weather is hot and sunny.

Udder The part of a cow where milk is made.

Vat A large bowl for holding liquids.

Index